AMAZING HOCKEY STORIES

ALEX OVECHKIN

Lorna Schultz Nicholson

Illustrations by D. A. Bishop

Scholastic Canada Ltd.
Toronto New York London Auckland Sydney
Mexico City New Delhi Hong Kong Buenos Aires

To all young hockey players . . . always enjoy playing
this game as much as Alex Ovechkin! — *L.S.N.*

Scholastic Canada Ltd.
604 King Street West, Toronto, Ontario M5V 1E1, Canada

Scholastic Inc.
557 Broadway, New York, NY 10012, USA

Scholastic Australia Pty Limited
PO Box 579, Gosford, NSW 2250, Australia

Scholastic New Zealand Limited
Private Bag 94407, Botany, Manukau 2163, New Zealand

Scholastic Children's Books
Euston House, 24 Eversholt Street, London NW1 1DB, UK

www.scholastic.ca

Library and Archives Canada Cataloguing in Publication
Title: Alex Ovechkin / Lorna Schultz Nicholson ; illustrations by D.A. Bishop.
Names: Schultz Nicholson, Lorna, author. | Bishop, D. A. (David A.), illustrator.
Description: Series statement: Amazing hockey stories
Identifiers: Canadiana 20210160195 | ISBN 9781443187718 (softcover)
Subjects: LCSH: Ovechkin, Alexander, 1985- —Juvenile literature. |
LCSH: Hockey players—Russia (Federation)—Biography—Juvenile literature.
Classification: LCC GV848.5.O95 S39 2021 | DDC j796.962092—dc23

Photos ©: cover: David Becker/NHLI via Getty Images; background:
Nick Merkulov/Shutterstock; 5 : Bruce Bennett/Getty Images;
18: Dave Sandford/Hockey Hall of Fame; 20: Vladimir Bezzubov;
22: Karl DeBlaker/AP Images; 25: Josh Holberg/Hockey Hall of Fame;
36: Mitchell Layton/Getty Images; 48: Bruce Bennett/Getty Images;
55: Roy K. Miller/Icon Sportswire via Getty Images; 60: Jonathan Newton/
The Washington Post via Getty Images; 64: Alex Brandon/AP Images.

6 5 4 3 2 1   Printed in China 62   21 22 23 24 25

FSC
www.fsc.org
MIX
Paper from
responsible sources
FSC® C020056

CONTENTS

LIVING LEGEND

Dangerous. Dazzling. Durable. These are all words used to describe the Russian-born hockey player Alexander Ovechkin. On February 22, 2020, Alex wowed hockey fans around the world by scoring his 700th National Hockey League goal. Right off the faceoff, Alex blasted the puck to the back of the net with his powerful release.

Over his many years in the NHL, Alex's bullet shot has shocked many a goalie. When he scored his milestone 700th goal, his famous gap-toothed smile stretched from ear to ear, and "Ovi" did his usual celebration: lifting one leg up, his arms punching the air. Alex is just the eighth player in NHL history to reach 700 goals, and he is the second fastest getting there. Only Wayne Gretzky has reached this amazing accomplishment in fewer games.

A dominant force in the NHL, Alex has won just about every bit of hardware there is to win, including the Maurice "Rocket" Richard Trophy. It's awarded to the player who scores the most goals in the regular season, and Alex won it an astounding nine times in 14 years!

He has earned the nicknames "the Great Eight" and "Alexander the Great," as well as "Ovi." In addition to being a singular talent, he has been *the* franchise player for the Washington Capitals — a player the Caps saw as valuable enough to build their team around.

ALEX ABOUT TO SCORE HIS 700TH NHL GOAL IN A GAME AGAINST THE NEW JERSEY DEVILS.

Athletic greatness seems to run in Alex's family. His mother, Tatyana, was a famous Russian basketball player, winning Olympic gold medals in 1976 and 1980 with the Soviet Union National Team. She played professional basketball for Moscow's Dynamo Sports Society, a sports and fitness organization. His father, Mikhail, was a soccer player for Dynamo, which is where they met.

Alexander Mikhailovich Ovechkin was born on September 17, 1985, the youngest of three boys. The eldest, Sergei, was fourteen when Alex was born, and his brother Mikhail was three.

Sergei had been a wrestler, but didn't make the national team. Mikhail lost interest in sports when he was in his teens. Would Alex be the "brat" — Russian for brother — who would be the star athlete, perhaps on a basketball court or a soccer pitch?

GROWING UP IN THE USSR

There weren't many luxuries. At that time, Russia was under the rule of the Union of Soviet Socialist Republics, or the USSR. The Communist government had strict rules and gave its citizens few freedoms. Alex's mother managed to get a few extra privileges because of her Olympic gold medals. She received things that weren't offered to other families, including fruit in the winter, soccer balls and sometimes even gum! Alex grew up in the suburbs outside of Moscow, living in a neighbourhood of rundown apartment buildings. Alex's public school had a number (#596) instead of a name, as well as a principal who enforced army-like discipline.

Russians were not allowed to live or work in any other country. They could try to defect, or secretly leave the country, but they would never be able to return. Defecting was illegal and dangerous. The government's tough rules even applied to hockey. The sport was very popular in Russia, and its national team was one of the best in the world. But star players from the USSR were not allowed to leave to play in the NHL.

In the early 1990s, life changed in a big way for the Russian people. There was a change in government: it was no longer under strict Communist rule. This meant Russian hockey players could now play in the NHL without having to defect. There was hope for those who were good enough to get there.

HOCKEY?

Alex's family wasn't a hockey family. Even so, his favourite toy was a hockey stick. Alex carried it everywhere. If hockey was on television, he wouldn't let anyone change the channel. Alex's mother noticed that "Sasha" — her nickname for him — was naturally athletic. When he first played basketball, he could handle the ball properly, and he had good technical soccer skills, too. Of course, she wanted him to follow in her Olympic footsteps and play basketball.

Alex didn't try skating until he was seven — a late start. The first time he stepped on the ice he fell, as other kids zoomed by. Skating was hard, and he wasn't sure he liked it. His parents weren't sure they wanted him to play hockey either. It seemed like a tough sport when there were others to choose. After playing a few times, Alex quit. But there was one person who still thought he should be a hockey player — his big brother Sergei. He encouraged Alex — or "Toad," as Sergei called him — to try again. Since their parents were busy in their jobs, Sergei offered to take eight-year-old Toad back to play hockey at the Dynamo Sports Society.

THE TRAINING BEGINS

So Alex stepped back on the ice. Compared to the other boys, he struggled. He could hardly skate, and they were doing crossovers. He even got benched at practice because he couldn't skate backwards. But Sergei encouraged him to keep at it. Alex stuck it out and started to put more work in. He wanted to play in a real game, but the coach wouldn't put him in, not even when they were leading one 8–1. At the next game, Alex was still warming the bench. His mother threatened to pull him, but he begged her to let him stay. Finally, the coach put him out for the third period. Alex has hardly left the ice since.

His mother soon saw that Alex had a passion for the sport. As an elite athlete herself, she knew that to be successful, he would need some help to catch up. She decided to use her influence as a former star of the Dynamo Sports Society basketball team to get it for him. Even then, Alex was rejected by an experienced coach, so his parents turned to a new coach named Vyacheslav Kirillov. He was just starting out, but Coach Kirillov agreed to train Alex.

Unfortunately a late start wasn't the only struggle young Alex would face.

BETTER AND BETTER

Being on the ice up to three times a day paid off. Alex soon became a sharpshooter and a powerful skater. The year he was 12, Alex was among the top goal scorers for his team. Right before the last game of the season, Alex's father pointed out that Russian-born NHL superstar Pavel Bure's record at the same age was 56 points in one season. Alex had 53 points. Bure was one of Alex's personal heroes. He got on the ice and scored six times to break Bure's record.

Alex continued to improve through his early teens. He became so strong that he started playing professional hockey for HC Dynamo Moscow of the Russian Superleague when he was just 16. (This league became the Kontinental Hockey league, or KHL, in 2008.) Unlike North America, where a junior hockey player's oldest competitor would be 20, Alex played against grown men. Some of the players were in their 30s and had their own families!

But just as Alex was starting to have professional success, he had to deal with more heartache. Coach Kirillov passed away from heart issues. Even Alex's own father said Coach Kirillov "was like a second father for Sasha" and that Alex owed him everything.

The work Alex did with Coach Kirillov had helped him tremendously. By the end of four years playing with Dynamo, he was a regular on the scoresheet. But it was with the Russian National Team that Alex really started to get noticed . . . by NHL scouts.

THE INTERNATIONAL STAGE

The same year that Alex started playing in the Superleague, he was asked to be on the Russian Under-17 National Team. They would be playing in the International Ice Hockey Federation's World Under-17 Hockey Challenge in Canada, from December 29, 2001, to January 4, 2002. The Russians were first up against Finland in Selkirk, Manitoba. Scouts huddled in the cold arena with one hundred or so fans. Programs were nowhere to be found, so Alex's face wasn't splashed around anywhere. They even spelled his name wrong on the scoresheet — Alexandre Overchrine!

But none of that mattered. The moment he stepped on the ice, the scouts sat up in their seats. Who was this Russian dynamo? Alex scored 12 goals in the tournament, 6 more than any other player. He wound up with 14 points, even though Russia came sixth overall. People began buzzing about the Russian sharpshooter who always seemed to be in the right position to score. Scouts said he was "passionate" and he "looks to score and shoots a ton."

The Russian National Team soon asked Alex to play for them again. The 2002 IIHF Ice Hockey U18 Championship was in Slovakia that April. The Russians had a better result this time, winning their division. They faced Team USA in the final, losing 3–1 but capturing the silver medal. Alex earned the most points in the tournament with 14 goals and 4 assists . . . and he was still only 16 years old.

IN THE SPOTLIGHT

Now he was really creating a buzz with scouts and sports agents. There were many who wanted to represent this young phenom, figuring he would be a superstar one day. One after the other, they travelled to Russia to try to win Alex over. The entire Ovechkin family attended dinners at fancy restaurants in Moscow, but it was Alex's mother who asked most of the questions and made the demands. Alex finally signed a contract — his sights were on the NHL, even if he wasn't quite old enough yet.

In the meantime, Alex still loved playing for his country. When the Russian Under-20 coaches asked him to play in the 2003 IIHF World Junior Hockey Championships, to be held in Canada, he quickly agreed. He wanted to win the gold for Russia.

In the first game, against the USA on December 26, 2002, in Sydney, Nova Scotia, Alex scored a hat trick to lead Russia to a 5–1 victory. Russia went on to win their next two round-robin games. Then they were headed to Halifax for the semifinal — and hopefully the gold-medal game. When the team arrived in Halifax, there was a press conference for Alex. He could speak only a few words of English, so he used a translator. Alex said his goal wasn't so much to show what he could do, but to win the gold medal. Then he was asked a personal question, "What is your brother Sergei's influence?" Alex and his family were usually very private about Sergei and how his death had affected them, but Alex answered, "Every game I play, I think of him."

Russia went on to beat Finland in the semifinal matchup by a score of 4–1. Then it was time for Russia to face Canada in the final. Russia was favoured to win and took an early lead, but Canada answered back with a goal to tie it at the end of the first. When

Canada scored in the second period, taking the lead, the Canadian fans cheered wildly — but this only inspired the Russians to do better. In the third period, they came back to score two goals for a 3–2 victory. Alex lined up with his teammates and proudly sang the Russian national anthem. He had earned gold for his country.

Alex left Halifax with his medal in his luggage and went back to Russia to play with his Dynamo team. He had another good year, finishing with 8 goals and 7 assists in 40 games. Alex continued training hard. His draft year was coming up in 2004, and he wanted to be ready.

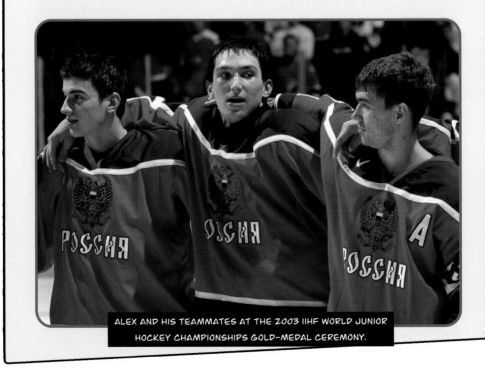

ALEX AND HIS TEAMMATES AT THE 2003 IIHF WORLD JUNIOR HOCKEY CHAMPIONSHIPS GOLD-MEDAL CEREMONY.

DRAFTED . . . TWICE?

But in the 2003 NHL Entry Draft, something funny happened. The event in Nashville, Tennessee, was winding down. The first draft picks had already donned their jerseys, and the stands were starting to empty. Then, for the 265th pick, the Florida Panthers announced that they would choose Alex Ovechkin. But how could this be? A player had to be 18 years old as of September 15 to be drafted into the NHL, and Alex's birthday was September 17. Florida tried to back up their choice by saying Alex which would be 18 years old *if* leap years were factored in. This produced a lot of chuckles . . . and then Florida was told to pick another player. All joking aside, there were many NHL teams who had serious interest in the young Russian star.

For the entire 2003–04 season, NHL scouts and team managers were watching the now 18-year-old Alex with the possibility of drafting him on their minds. He again played in the 2004 World Junior Championships in Helsinki, Finland. Although Alex wowed the fans with five goals and two assists, the Russians were beat out 3–2 by the home team in the quarter-final and ended up with a disappointing fifth-place finish.

ALEX WITH COACH VLADIMIR KRIKUNOV OF THE MOSCOW DYNAMO.

The loss, however, didn't stop many sports pundits and broadcasters from speculating that Alex would be the first pick at the next NHL Entry Draft. Others thought it would be fellow Russian player Evgeni Malkin. The Pittsburgh Penguins, coming in last place in the Eastern Conference after a disastrous season, had the greatest chance of getting the first pick. The Washington Capitals, on the other hand, had only 14 percent odds for the same pick. When the ping-pong balls were drawn, the winner of the draft lottery was the lucky Washington Capitals.

THE ACTUAL DRAFT

But, before the draft itself, there was the NHL Scouting Combine to deal with. It's an evaluation of players that involves four gruelling days of fitness tests and interviews. Even the thought of a combine makes many players nervous, afraid they will make a bad impression. But Alex showed up looking relaxed and definitely himself. Unlike the other young players in their suits and dress shirts, Alex wore bright red jeans with suspenders hanging down, a black T-shirt that stretched across his bulging muscles, and red wrestling shoes. Even though he still didn't speak much English, he made an impression with his positive, polite and upbeat attitude and the non-stop smile that would soon become a trademark.

Alex excelled beyond expectations. He came in well above average in bench press, standing long jump, vertical jump and chin-ups. But when he got on the stationary bike for the aerobic test, he skyrocketed past all the other players. He already had the heart and lungs of an elite professional athlete.

The draft took place on June 26, 2004, at the RBC Center in Raleigh, North Carolina. To virtually no one's surprise, the Washington Capitals selected

Alex as their number-one pick. When they called his name, he hugged his mother and father, who had travelled over from Russia. Grinning, he walked up to the stage to put on the Capitals jersey. The commentators said he was a complete player with a winning personality on and off the ice. Alex smiled big for the camera.

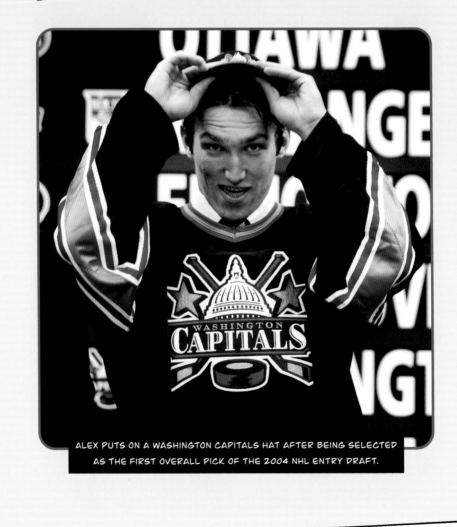

ALEX PUTS ON A WASHINGTON CAPITALS HAT AFTER BEING SELECTED AS THE FIRST OVERALL PICK OF THE 2004 NHL ENTRY DRAFT.

After he left the stage, he spoke to a reporter. Determined to practise his English, Alex gave the interview without a translator. When asked how he was feeling about being the first overall draft pick, he said, "I very happy." Then, asked about the future of his hockey career, he replied, "My brother want me to play hockey," and then, "Thank you very much." Sometimes Alex gave answers that had nothing to do with the question because he didn't quite understand it. But he kept trying, and if he made a mistake, he just laughed it off.

DEBUT DELAYED

Unfortunately, what was supposed to be his debut season in the NHL wasn't funny at all. There was a dispute about how to manage player salaries, and the players were locked out for the entire 2004–05 season. Alex was disappointed. He had been looking forward to playing with and against other NHL players. Instead, he headed back to Russia and the Dynamo team. At least he was playing.

Alex got a taste of what it might be like to be in the NHL when he was named to Russia's 2004 World Cup of Hockey roster. The tournament was to begin at the end of August, and some of the best hockey players in the world were competing in it, including many top NHL players. On the ice, Alex proved he was ready for "the Show," giving and taking hits, as well as shooting and skating with the big boys. Off the ice, he tried to do interviews by himself, only using a translator if needed. The Russian National Team were in the North American grouping at the World Cup and ended up losing in the quarter-finals to the USA by a 5–3 score. But the tournament was not a complete loss for Alex. He was that much more ready for his NHL debut.

With the lockout lasting a full season, Dynamo allowed Alex to play in the 2005 IIHF World Junior Championship in North Dakota. Canada had a team stacked with NHL players, including the most talked-about, Sidney Crosby. When Crosby played at the 2004 World Juniors, Russia and Canada didn't face off against each other. But this year was different. It was the draft year for "Sid the Kid" and he was looking to make a big impression. Crosby seemed to make it his mission to check Alex when they were on the ice together, knowing that the Russian player needed to be stopped or he would score. Between that and a talent-heavy team, Canada was victorious, giving the Russians a bit of a beating with a 6–1 final score in the gold-medal game. Alex still ended up third in the scoring race with 11 (7 goals and 4 assists), just after Patrice Bergeron, who topped the list with 13, and Ryan Getzlaf, at 12.

ALEX SALUTES THE CROWD AFTER RUSSIA'S 6–1 LOSS TO CANADA IN THE GOLD-MEDAL GAME ON JANUARY 4, 2005.

Alex went on to finish another great year with Dynamo. In 37 games, he scored 13 goals, had 13 assists and helped them win the Russian Superleague playoffs, where he earned another 8 points! When spring arrived, it was time for the 2005 World Championships, taking place in Austria. Again, many international teams included top NHL players, and the competition was fierce. Near the end of the tournament, Canada nipped a win from Russia in the semifinals. But Russia bounced back, beating Sweden 6–3 to capture the bronze medal. Once again, 19-year-old Alex shone, cracking the top 10 in scoring for the entire tournament with 5 goals and 3 assists.

Alex had proven that he was more than ready for the big leagues.

WHAT WAS ALEX'S FAVOURITE HOCKEY TEAM WHEN HE WAS YOUNG?

THE PITTSBURGH PENGUINS!

THE ROOKIE

Alex couldn't wait for his rookie year with the Washington Capitals. As the first pick in the 2004 draft, people would be watching him. But he wasn't the only first pick about to start his rookie season. The lockout had created an interesting situation . . . there were two. At the 2005 NHL Entry Draft, it was no surprise when the Pittsburgh Penguins, who had finally nabbed that first selection, picked Crosby. Everyone had been talking about the hot new star from Cole Harbour, Nova Scotia. Now both Alex and Crosby would have their rookie years at the same time! The sports pundits were abuzz. Which rookie would come flying out of the gates when the NHL finally started up in October?

CANTALOUPES AND CORN FLAKES

When Alex hit the Capitals training camp in August, he was like a kid at an amusement park. Everything was new, exciting and so much fun! At a lunch he met the team's owner for the first time . . . and ate an entire cantaloupe. He'd never seen one back in Russia. During a visit to the general manager's house, they went for a long bike ride. Alex was so fit he completely outpaced his companion. By the time the general manager arrived back home, sweaty and exhausted, Alex was deep into a road hockey game with the GM's kids.

By now, Alex had a few more English words under his belt — including Corn Flakes, his new favourite breakfast — but he was still learning. After his first training session, he wrote down the names of all his teammates on the whiteboard in the dressing room. Then Alex practised reading them out loud. He did okay . . . until he got to the name Eminger. He just couldn't pronounce it, and the more he tried, the funnier it became. He got all the other players in on the fun. When Caps coach Glen Hanlon walked into the dressing room, everyone was laughing along with Alex. Coach Hanlon said, "I realized that this was no shrinking violet here. A 20-year-old kid had taken control of the room."

WHY DOES ALEX WEAR #8?

IT WAS THE NUMBER HIS MOTHER WORE WHEN SHE PLAYED BASKETBALL.

GET READY, GET SET . . .

Alex proved himself in training camp, skating hard and showing that he could shoot and score. Capitals defenceman Mathieu Biron said, "In an intra-team game at the very start of training camp, Alex scored a goal and you could see something really unique in his eyes. It was like a volcano about to explode with joy . . . I had never seen a player who liked to score so much. Whether in practice or in exhibition games, there was not a single goal that did not please him. He's like a kid at Christmas every time." Camp ended, and Alex's name was a definite YES on the roster. He was also put on the first power-play unit.

Wednesday, October 5, 2005, was a big day. After 548 days without seeing their team play, Capitals fans were starving for the season to begin — and looking for a reason to hope. They'd had enough of a team who lost more than they won and rarely saw the playoffs. Was this young Russian as good as people said? Was he the franchise player the Capitals could build their team around? Today was the day they'd find out.

HITTING THE HIGHLIGHT REEL

Alex showed Caps fans and management they had a superstar in the making. On January 13, 2006, in his 43rd game, he hit another milestone. The Caps were playing against the Mighty Ducks of Anaheim, and the first period went by with no scoring. Early in the second, Alex skated through the traffic and popped in the first goal of the game for the Caps.

The Ducks answered back, and the score was 1–1. The tie was short-lived because Alex once again got in the Ducks' zone, and this time he did a curl and drag before blasting the puck into the back of the net. With less than three minutes left in the third, the Ducks scored again to tie the game. The buzzer sounded. It was going to overtime. At 3:04 of the overtime period, young Alex circled around a few Ducks . . . and wheeled in to score the OT winner. His teammates hugged him, knowing he'd won it for the Caps — with his first NHL hat trick, no less!

Three days later, the Caps were in Phoenix facing the Coyotes. Alex scored the first goal of the game and picked up an assist in the second period. The Caps were up 5–1 in the third period and set for an easy win. That didn't stop Alex from doing what he loves to do: score goals. In a defining moment,

Alex stormed down the ice and into the Coyotes' zone using his strong stickhandling skills. A Coyotes defenceman tripped him up, and he tumbled to the ice. As he was sliding along the ice on his back, and with only one hand on his stick, he reached for the puck. He smacked at it, sending it into the net on a backhand! Jaws dropped. It was an unbelievable goal, and it has been played over and over in sports broadcasts. It's been called one of the greatest ever.

About a month after his highlight-reel goal, Alex was selected for the Russian Olympic Team at the 2006 Winter Olympics in Turin, Italy. It was another dream come true. The tournament started off well. The Russians put on a good show in the round robin, losing only one of the four games they played. In the quarter-final matchup, they faced Canada. Alex scored the first goal, which proved to be the game-winner, and the Russians ended up taking it 2–0. They advanced to a semifinal against Finland, which Russia lost. They also lost the bronze-medal game. Alex was determined to represent his country on the Olympic stage again one day. He was proud to wear the jersey of his home country.

CROSBY CHASES "OVI" DOWN THE ICE IN A GAME ON FEBRUARY II, 2006.

OVECHKIN OR CROSBY?

After the Olympics, Alex returned to Washington and the NHL to finish off his high-flying rookie year. The big question for sports enthusiasts: Who would win the Calder Memorial Trophy as the NHL's top rookie — Alex or Crosby? Both had dominated on offence and were nominated along with Dion Phaneuf, who was playing defence with the Calgary Flames. But Alex had a real knack for scoring goals, and by season's end, he'd tallied an amazing 52 goals and 54 assists, amassing 106 points. Crosby wasn't far behind him with 39 goals and 63 assists for 102 points. Who would take the hardware for Rookie of the Year?

The voting by the Professional Hockey Writers Association wasn't even close. Alex got 125 out of 129 first-place votes! His impressive 52 goals had steered the voters in his direction. And no one could forget that highlight-reel goal in Phoenix — or all those hard hits. Along with the Calder Memorial Trophy, he won the Kharlamov Trophy, given to the best Russian player in the NHL. Alex made the NHL First All-Star Team, the first rookie to do so since Chicago's Ed Belfour in the 1990–91 season. He also made the NHL All-Rookie All-Star Team. It was a fantastic first year . . . but the Capitals did not make the playoffs, and that was something Alex desperately wanted.

WHAT ELSE IS SPECIAL ABOUT THE NUMBER 8 FOR ALEX?

HIS SON SERGEI WAS BORN ON 08/18/18.

PLAYOFF DREAMS

The 2006–07 season didn't exactly go as Alex hoped. In 82 games, he had 46 goals, finishing shy of the 50 he was aiming for. His 46 assists made for a total of 92 points on the season, putting him in 13th place in the league. That was well short of Crosby's whopping 120-point season. More than that though, the Caps again didn't make the playoffs.

Disappointed, Alex went home to Russia. He had fulfilled his dream of making the NHL, but now he had another: to win a Stanley Cup. He trained very hard in the off-season. There was also some business to take care of. His entry-level contract was in its last year. Alex decided to negotiate without an agent, and, with his parents, met with the Caps' GM in France. The meeting ended without a deal.

Alex returned to Washington in the fall, determined to help his team reach the playoffs. The Caps didn't have a great start to their 2007–08 season, with few wins. But Alex was still racking up goals and assists. After a coaching change in November, the team started winning more games. Maybe they could pull it off, but they needed the help of their young star. Would they have it?

Alex's contract was up. Negotiations had been going on since the summer and nothing was certain. Again, with just his parents in the room to help him, they signed a record deal for a 13-year contract extension! This meant he would be with the Caps until the 2020–21 season. It was clear the team saw him as a franchise player, one who would be key to their success over the next decade . . . and beyond. Alex could not have been happier. He loved Washington and his teammates.

The deal was big news, but Alex took it in his usual easygoing stride. At the press conference to announce it, he was asked about the amount of money he was getting paid. He humbly said, "I feel I have everything." The owner of the Capitals smiled and joked, "A front tooth?" Alex joked back, "Maybe razor." Everyone laughed because he was known for his unshaven face and shaggy hair. But today, in a new suit and with his hair neatly brushed, he cracked back, "I'm still looking good." On a more serious note, he added, "I know it's extra pressure, but I have to play the same."

The Caps were having a good season. It looked as if the playoffs were in reach. Right before the February trade deadline, they added veteran player

Sergei Fedorov. Fedorov was one of the first Russian players to join the NHL, one of the best players in the world and one of Alex's heroes. Having Fedorov on the team was fun for Alex. Not only did he get to play with his hero, but he got to speak — and joke around — in Russian in the dressing room.

It looked like having Fedorov on the Capitals was the boost Alex needed. At the end of the season, he had scored his most goals ever, with 65, and earned 47 assists, for a total of 112 points. That was the highest total in the league. More importantly, the Caps were the Southeast Division champions and came third in the Eastern Conference with 94 points. They were headed to the playoffs, meeting the Philadelphia Flyers in the first round. Would Alex see his new dream come true?

ALEX HAS BEEN ON THE COVER OF EA SPORTS' NHL 07 AND NHL 21, AS WELL AS NHL 2K10, BUT HIS FAVOURITE GAME IS CANDY CRUSH!

THE TROPHY CASE

After getting the gold at the World Championship, Alex's winning streak continued. At the 2008 NHL Awards in June, he completely cleaned up! He won the Art Ross Trophy, the Hart Memorial Trophy, the Rocket Richard Trophy and the Lester B. Pearson Award for most outstanding player in the regular season. Alex became the first player in NHL history to win these four major trophies. He also picked up another Kharlamov Trophy to add to his growing hardware collection.

CONTINUING TO CLIMB

Alex was impatient for the 2008–09 season to start. He missed two games in October, visiting his sick grandfather in Russia. But after he returned and the season was underway, Washington gained a great burst of energy. With Alex leading their scoring, they won the Southeast Division and came second in the Eastern Conference, with 108 points. At the end of the season, Alex was once again the NHL's top goal scorer, with 56 goals and 54 assists for a total of 110 points. And that was with only 79 games played. The Capitals were off to the playoffs again.

EPIC BATTLES

Alex had a second chance for a Stanley Cup. He and the Capitals faced the New York Rangers in the first round. The Caps had a rocky start, falling behind in the series 3–1. But they battled back with three straight victories and were off to the second round . . . against Crosby and the Pittsburgh Penguins, in a much talked-about matchup. Again it was the Penguins, led by their young superstar, versus the Capitals, with theirs. Alex needed to put his head down and play hockey, not listen to the pundits. The teams came out flying in the first game, and both Alex and Crosby scored a goal. But it was the Caps who edged out the Penguins 3–2.

The second game was one for the NHL history books, and had all the intensity of a Stanley Cup Final. The first period saw Crosby doing what he does best — hanging out at the side of the net, looking for a pass or a rebound to flip over the goalie's shoulder. It was 1–0 for Pittsburgh at the end of the first. Only two minutes into the second period, it was time for Alex to do what *he* does best. He rifled a blasting shot from mid-ice to tie it up. Crosby retaliated, scoring his second goal of the night on another chip shot from the side of the net. The game of ping-pong continued when David Steckel scored for the Caps. Off they went to the dressing room at the end of the second, tied 2–2.

In the first half of the third, both teams rushed up and down the ice, with the goalies making acrobatic saves. At 12:33 into the period, Alex circled, getting open, and when the puck came his way, he nailed a one-timer. The red light lit up. Alex and Crosby were both on the scoresheet with two apiece. Less than three minutes later, Alex saw a loose puck slide out from along the right boards, and he exploded toward it, picking it up and pushing past the Pittsburgh defenceman. He let go another booming shot . . . GOAL! It was a hat trick for Alex, and Washington was leading 4–2. The Caps fans went wild, throwing their hats on the ice, as Crosby stood by his bench, anxious for another chance. With less than a minute left in the period, Pittsburgh was on the power play and Crosby was back by the side of the net. The puck came his way. He shot. Big save. Shot again. Another big save. Shot again. And then . . . it was third time lucky for Crosby. The Caps ended up winning the game 4–3, but both Alex and Crosby had scored hat tricks. This was exactly the superstar showdown the media had been buzzing about.

The epic battle lasted seven games, with three going into overtime. Unfortunately for the Caps, the Penguins won game seven, with Crosby getting yet another hat trick. He finished the series with 13 points — but Alex had 14, the highest single-series point total since the 1995 playoffs.

Alex cleaned up again at the 2009 NHL Awards. But the trophy he really wanted was the Stanley Cup.

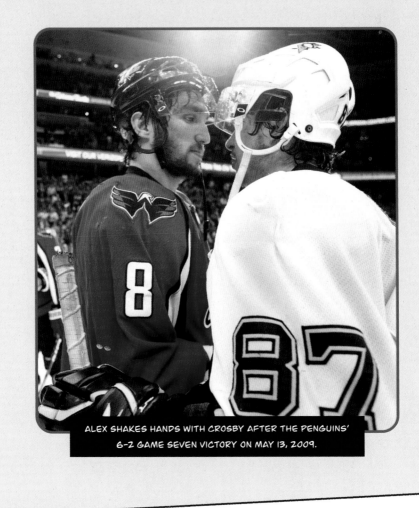

ALEX SHAKES HANDS WITH CROSBY AFTER THE PENGUINS' 6-2 GAME SEVEN VICTORY ON MAY 13, 2009.

THE FRANCHISE PLAYER

On January 5, 2010, Alex was made the captain of the Capitals in recognition of his stellar play on the ice and his leadership skills in the dressing room. He wore the "C" with pride and helped the Caps make the playoffs for a third straight year. Unfortunately, their playoff run was halted after the first round, when they were bested by the Montreal Canadiens in seven games. Still, Alex wound up with a solid 50-goal season, and at the 2010 NHL Awards, he was recognized by his fellow players with the Ted Lindsay Award, and he won his fifth Kharlamov Trophy.

The 2010–11 season found Alex hitting some big milestones. On March 9, 2011, he earned his 600th point, in a 5–0 victory over the Edmonton Oilers. Then on April 5, in a game against the Toronto Maple Leafs, he scored his 300th career goal, becoming the sixth-youngest and seventh-fastest player to do so. The Caps again made the playoffs. In the first round, they bested the New York Rangers four games to one. But they were swept by the Tampa Bay Lightning in the second round. It was like a curse — they just couldn't get to the Eastern Conference Final!

CLOSE, BUT NOT CLOSE ENOUGH

The 2012–13 season saw a lot of drama. The season didn't start in the fall because the players were locked out by the team owners over a labour dispute. Not willing to lose time on the ice, Alex went back to Russia and the Dynamo team, who were thrilled to have the superstar back. When NHL play finally resumed in January, Alex roared back with it. He was the top scorer again, with 32 goals, and he had 24 assists for 56 points in just 48 games. The Capitals advanced to the playoffs, but they didn't make it past the first round.

The 2013–14 year was also a major disappointment. Yes, Alex won the Rocket Richard Trophy with 51 goals, but the Caps finished fifth in their division and they didn't advance further. Over the next three years, despite having success during the regular season, they had little luck in the playoffs. Each time the Caps won round one but lost in the conference semifinals.

It seemed Alex might be one of those great players who never reaches the Stanley Cup Final — just like legend Pavel Bure, Alex's childhood hero. Alex continued to have success on the ice though. In two of those three years, he won the Rocket Richard

Trophy. He'd been awarded the hardware a whopping six times now! But would he ever hoist the Stanley Cup above his head?

THE 2017-18 SEASON

It was Alex's 13th season with the Washington Capitals. At 32 years old, he still felt strong and healthy. Keen to improve on the previous season's 33 goals, he was pumped for the opening game against the Ottawa Senators. The third period saw the Caps behind 3–1 . . . until Alex scored a hat trick and they went on to win it. The next day he scored another hat trick — and then one more goal! It was exactly the start he was looking for.

On April 1, 2018, he played his 1,000th game with the Caps, beating the Penguins 3–1. When the season ended in April 2018, they had 105 points — short of their 120-point record, but still third in their division. It wasn't their regular-season domination like the previous two years, but they had made the playoffs. Alex was a huge contributor to their point total. He was the NHL's goal leader for the seventh time, with 49 goals and 38 assists.

Maybe this year the playoffs would be different?

A RIVAL RETURNS

In the first round, the Caps faced off against the Columbus Blue Jackets. In the first two games, Alex played hard hockey, with lots of hits, and he nailed two power-play goals in the second game. Both games went to OT, and Columbus came out victorious each time. Many were doubting the Caps. They'd dug a hole for themselves. Could they save the series? Washington would have to do better . . . and they did. The third game was a classic, going to two overtime periods — and the Caps came out the winner! This launched their comeback, and in game six, Alex potted two goals for the series win. Next up was an old playoff foe: the defending champions, the Pittsburgh Penguins.

In the first game, the Penguins were down by two but rallied with three goals in the third to take the game. The chatter started: the Caps were in their dreaded second round; the one they couldn't conquer. Washington rallied back to win the second and third games, taking a 2–1 lead in the series. But the Penguins weren't giving up. By now, both Alex and Crosby were veterans. Of course, Crosby had the experience of winning the Cup, and the Penguins tied up the series. In game five, the Caps got busy, taking a commanding lead and winning 6–3. Alex's scoring chances were huge. He always seemed to be in the right place at the right time. But Pittsburgh goalie Matt Murray was making incredible acrobatic saves.

Heading into game six up 3–2, the Caps desperately wanted the win to take the series. The Penguins needed to hang on to force a game seven. The first period was typical Caps versus Penguins action, with Alex and Crosby being fiercely competitive. Two minutes into the second period, the Caps scored first. Ten minutes later the Penguins tied it up . . . and the game ended tied at a goal apiece, heading into OT. Just five minutes into the overtime period, Alex saw the loose puck at centre ice. He picked it up, dug in his edges, and skated. Breaking out in front of him was teammate Evgeny Kuznetsov. Alex fired off a tape-to-tape pass, giving Kuznetsov a breakaway. And he nailed it! The Caps had broken their curse.

WHAT DID ALEX GET FOR HIS 30TH BIRTHDAY IN MOSCOW?

A SHEEP! "OVECHKA" MEANS "LITTLE SHEEP" IN RUSSIAN.

THE RUN FOR THE CUP

In Alex's first trip to the Eastern Conference Final, the Caps were up against the Tampa Bay Lightning. The start of the series saw Tampa with home-ice advantage, but Washington dominated, stealing both games with scores of 4–2 and 6–2. Alex was on the ice for big minutes, adding up hits and shots and points. They headed back to Washington looking for a win. But in a weird turn of events, Tampa stole both games back, with identical 4–2 scores. Back on home ice for game five, Tampa impressed their fans with a 3–2 win to pull ahead in the series. The plane back to Washington was quiet for the Caps. They wanted to give their fans something to cheer about, too.

What happened next was spectacular. In games six and seven, the Caps didn't allow a goal against, winning 3–0 and 4–0. The Capitals' goalie, Braden Holtby, made 53 consecutive saves in the two games, earning two shutouts — a huge feat. Hyped to win and move on to the Stanley Cup Final, Alex had picked up the first goal in game seven. When the series was over, Alex was interviewed. "I'm emotional right now," he said. "We've been waiting for this moment for a long time."

The Caps would be playing against a team that was making NHL history. The Vegas Golden Knights were an expansion team in their very first year, with no real superstars. But these underdogs had won the hearts of fans everywhere with their gritty and passionate play and were riding into the Stanley Cup Final with a huge amount of momentum.

ALEX CELEBRATES WITH HIS TEAMMATES AFTER WINNING GAME SEVEN OF THE 2018 EASTERN CONFERENCE FINAL.

TIME TO CELEBRATE!

The Stanley Cup wasn't the only trophy Alex won that day. At the end of game five, he was awarded the Conn Smythe Trophy, for MVP of the playoffs. But it was the Stanley Cup he skated around the ice with. All smiles, Alex held the trophy over his head and circled the rink. The celebration continued in the dressing room, with everyone singing "We Are the Champions." When it was Alex's turn to have the Stanley Cup during the off-season, he took it to Russia to show it off in his homeland and he spent the summer enjoying his moment.

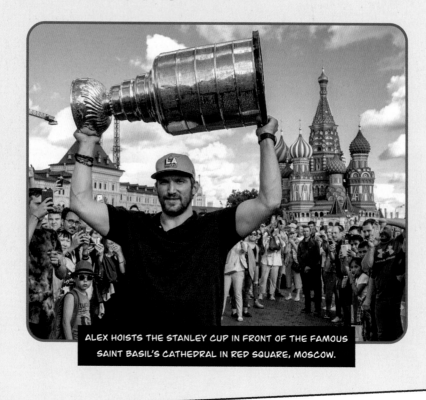

ALEX HOISTS THE STANLEY CUP IN FRONT OF THE FAMOUS SAINT BASIL'S CATHEDRAL IN RED SQUARE, MOSCOW.

ANOTHER TYPICAL SEASON

When Alex arrived back in Washington for training camp for the 2018–19 season, he was determined to repeat the victory. The Caps had a strong season, finishing with 104 points, and coming first in the Metropolitan Division and third overall in the Eastern Conference. Alex had scored an amazing 51 goals, again winning the Maurice "Rocket" Richard Trophy — his eighth! Even better, the Caps had a chance at another Stanley Cup.

The Capitals faced the Carolina Hurricanes in the first round. The Caps took an early 2–0 series lead, but the Canes fought back to even it up. It looked as if Washington would clinch the series after they won game five 6–0. The pesky Hurricanes didn't give up and tied the series, forcing a game seven. The Caps were all over the Canes in the first period, with Alex picking up an assist to make it 2–0. At the end of the second period, Washington was still leading 3–2. Carolina tied it in the third to take it to OT. Then the shocker happened. The Hurricanes defeated the Capitals in double overtime. Although Alex played well, with four goals and five assists in the series, the loss stung.

But there was always next year. Right?

UNUSUAL TIMES

The 2019–20 season started like many others. The Caps were doing well, winning more than they lost. In March, they were leading the Metropolitan Division and sitting third in the Eastern Conference. Alex was on target to score 50 goals, already tallying 48 goals and 19 assists in 69 games played. And then it all came to a crashing halt.

The COVID-19 virus was spreading around the world. It affected everything: schools, stores, businesses . . . and the world of sport. The NHL season was officially suspended on March 12, 2020, before the regular season was over. Hockey officials tried to figure out how they could have a Stanley Cup playoff. Maybe they could do it with no fans? No one wanted a repeat of the 1919 playoffs, which were held during an influenza pandemic. Those were cancelled right before the deciding game, after an outbreak made players sick.

The NHL finally decided to have two hub cities, Edmonton and Toronto, host the playoffs. The players would isolate together in a "bubble," avoiding contact with everybody but their coaches, trainers, team personnel and teammates. The Capitals made the top four in their division, earning a berth in the first round of the playoffs. They'd play the New York Islanders in the Toronto hub. Unfortunately, they lost the series four games to one, ending their season. This year, there would be no IIHF action, either. Everything was cancelled because of the pandemic. Alex flew home to Russia to wait for news on when the 2020–21 season would begin.

THE RECORD BOOKS

Alex has been a Washington Capitals franchise player, winning trophy after trophy, including the Stanley Cup. He loves his team, but he has kept a deep connection to his homeland. Every time the Caps got knocked out of the playoffs, Alex hopped on a plane and went to play for Russia. He's played in three World Junior Championships and thirteen World Championships, winning three gold medals, two silver and four bronze. He has played for Russia in three Olympic Games: 2006, 2010 and 2014. Alex wanted to play in the 2018 Games — and finally win the gold for his country — but the NHL did not allow its players to participate. It was a huge disappointment.

It's no surprise that Alex has two final goals: to finish his NHL career with Washington and then to return to Russia and play his victory lap with Dynamo. But he's not done yet! If Alex can play long enough, there is a chance he might catch Wayne Gretzky — "the Great One" — in most goals ever. Alex would need to hit Gretzky's 894 mark . . . and then score just one more goal to beat it.

Can he do it? He is Alex Ovechkin — "the Great Eight" — so anything is possible!

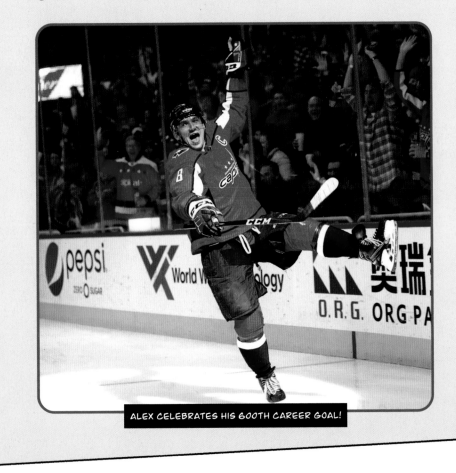

ALEX CELEBRATES HIS 600TH CAREER GOAL!